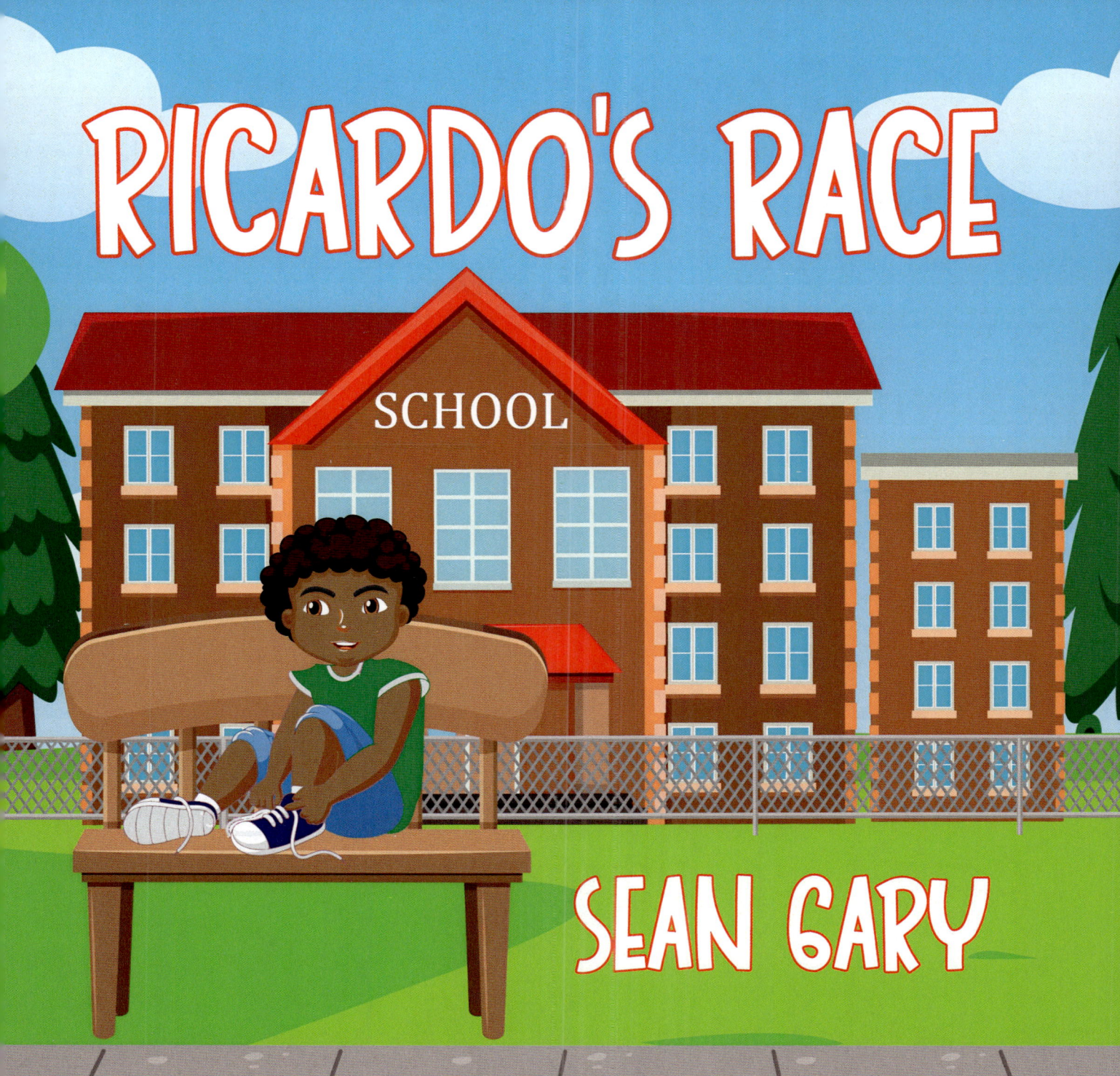

"And don't forget to put your race cars in the box labeled 'Toys'!" Ricardo's mom yelled up to him.

"Aww, Mom, why do we have to move anyway?"

Ricardo was packing up slowly because he didn't want to leave his friends. He also didn't want to leave his school.

Ricardo had spent the last few years racing every other kid in the school, and he had made a great name for himself.

"Ricardo G," they would call him that because he could run so fast. They even said he was from another galaxy.

Ron, Ricardo's big brother, was also very fast but didn't really like running so much. He loved his little brother Ricardo and would always tell him, "It's nice to be the fastest in the school but always remain humble."

Ron would also say, "Treat other people the way you want to be treated, and always, always, be a good sport!"

So the family moved to a new city in a new state. Ricardo and his big brother Ron had never been outside of Alabama before.

Ohio would be a new experience for sure, but leaving Alabama was also a journey!

Ron was excited to move. "I can't wait to see what the new kids are like!" he said.

But Ricardo was very nervous. He knew he was nervous, but he wasn't sure how to handle his emotion.

Ricardo grew more anxious about his first day of school at Terri Jamison Elementary. Maybe he had these feelings because he was in a new place, or maybe because he didn't know anyone yet. Ricardo thought about how he felt.

He didn't know how fast the other kids would be or if any of them would be nice to him. He just wanted at least one friend, so he didn't feel so alone.

Change was new to Ricardo. He wanted to stay emotionally stable, in a comfortable and familiar place. This move would truly challenge him because he would be outside of his comfort zone.

Before the two brothers knew it, it was time for school. As they approached the building Ron stopped outside of the school, to cheer his brother up.

Then Ron walked his brother Ricardo into the building. As the boys entered the hallway, they saw so many other kids who looked different than they did.

"Wow," Ricardo said to his brother. "Everyone looks so different."

Some kids were taller than he had expected. There were all kinds of different races of people, and Ricardo felt even more alone. He just wanted something or someone to connect with.

In a playing manner, Ron flicked his brother on the arm and said, "Hey, the differences are not a bad thing, little brother. We are all different in some way or another. Just be open to learning about other people's differences, and you just might be able to learn something from them."

"Then also look for the similarities," Ron continued. "It's a big world, but if you embrace the differences and enjoy the similarities, you will be just fine. I bet one of these guys loves to race. Watch, you will see!" Then Ron dropped Ricardo off and left to get to his school.

"Hey man! You are the new kid, right?" said a voice from behind Ricardo. "My name is Ari. Our teacher told us about you. It's Ricardo, right?"

Ari came closer and threw her arm around Ricardo as if they were already best friends. "You and I are in Mrs. LeShell's class! Check your sheet."

"Maybe, I think so," Ricardo said with a very shy voice. "Let me check my paper."

"I guess you are right!" Ricardo smiled.

They continued to walk through the hallway. All the nervous emotions Ricardo had felt were beginning to go away. This isn't that bad, he thought to himself.

Not too long ago, he had been so nervous about everything, and now he was happy to have someone help him out.

"Hey, Ari! Did you see that race last night?" a voice yelled from across the hallway.

Ari leaned over to Ricardo and said, "Just ignore him. That's Jace; he's the fastest kid in the school!"

"My brother Kaleb used to be the fastest," Ari added. "Kaleb was so fast he would give other students a head start. He was really nice like that!"

Ricardo asked, "What happened to Kaleb?"

"Oh, he's in middle school now," Ari answered. "But now Jace is in the top spot. Don't let his short legs fool you; Jace is really quick! But he's also mean to the other racers and can be a real bully sometimes."

"What race was he talking about? Ricardo asked Ari.

"Oh, our principal hosts these huge races every month!" Ari explained. "Principal Peaks, she's so cool! Everyone comes out to the race. It's like the biggest event in the school!"

"If you race," Ari continued, "everyone in school knows. But if you are the fastest in the school, everyone in the town knows."

"Wow, that's really cool! Do you race, Ari?" Ricardo asked.

"I used to. I was very fast, but nah, man, you could call me more like a —"

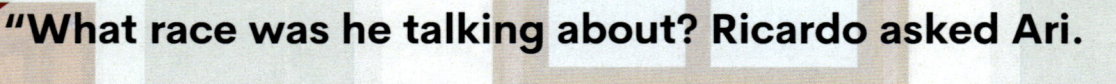

"Like a slugster! Cause she's slow as a SLUUUG!" Cairo interrupted Ari, laughing.

Cairo was Ari's best friend, and he always had something really silly to say. Cairo teased Ari like a big brother would tease his little sister.

"COACH!" replied Ari. "That's what I was going to say, Ricardo. I'm a coach."

"Cairo is my strongest runner. But I help a few other kids as well." As Ari looked over at Cairo, she pointed her finger in his face, and Cairo swatted it away.

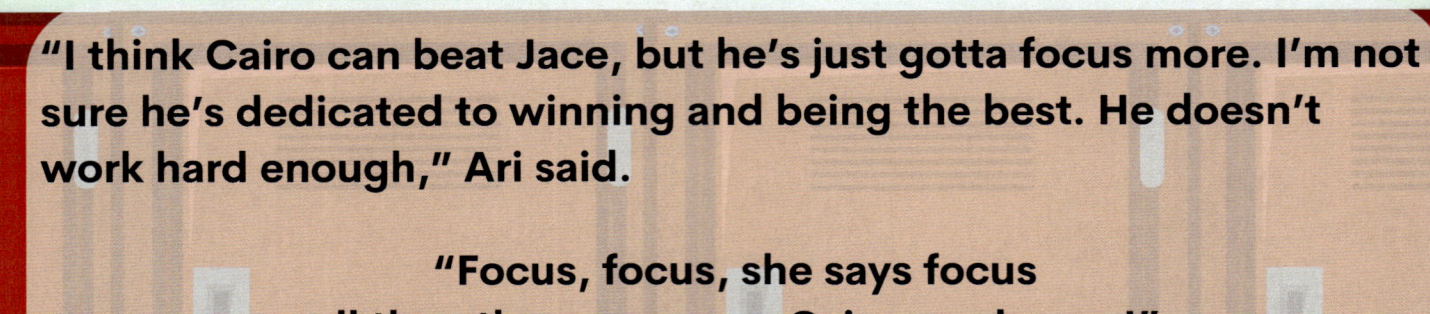

"I think Cairo can beat Jace, but he's just gotta focus more. I'm not sure he's dedicated to winning and being the best. He doesn't work hard enough," Ari said.

"Focus, focus, she says focus
all the other racers say Cairo smokes us!"

Cairo sang as he danced around the hallway.

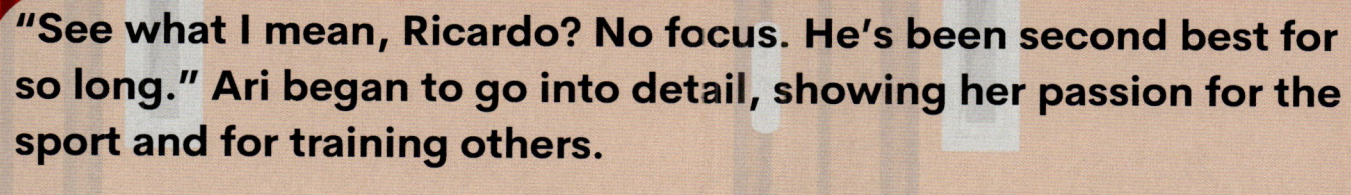

"See what I mean, Ricardo? No focus. He's been second best for so long." Ari began to go into detail, showing her passion for the sport and for training others.

"Nobody else is even close to beating Jace," Ari continued. "If Cairo worked hard, I bet he could beat Jace. Jace doesn't train or anything. He doesn't work hard; he's just really fast." Ari threw her hands up and then walked away.

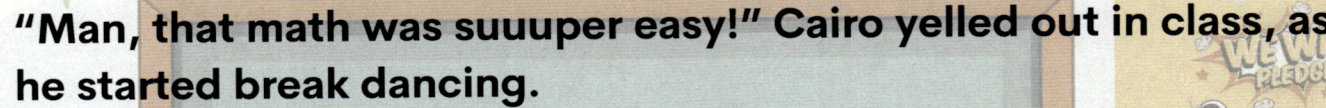

"Man, that math was suuuper easy!" Cairo yelled out in class, as he started break dancing.

Leaving their class, Cairo, Ari, and Ricardo headed to lunch.

"EASY? Oh yeah, is that why you got a D on that test then?" Ari snapped back playfully at Cairo. He stopped dancing. "But you did pretty well for your first week, Ricardo. An A-, that's impressive!"

"Thanks!" Ricardo replied.

He was much more comfortable at school now. He had made new friends, and they were always talking about racing. He never guessed that his nervous emotions would go away so quickly, and he now loved his school and new friends.

But more than anything, he was feeling excited because he was going to soon be racing again.

At lunch, Ricardo began to unpack his food. "I love these French fries, and this pizza is my favorite. Well, any pizza is my favorite." Ricardo said with great joy.

"I like pizza too," Cairo chimed in. "But I can't eat it as much as you do."

"Yeah, man," Ari said. "That food is not good for you."

Suddenly everyone in the whole lunchroom stopped and looked up as they heard a loud jingle over the PA system. BING, BING, BIIIIING.

"Hello, boys and girls," a sweet voice began. "I hope that you all are having a wonderful day so far! I just wanted to remind everyone of the upcoming race this week! Sign-ups are in the office. If you want to join the race, make sure you sign up before Thursday so we can have you on the list for Friday. Good luck to everyone, and remember to always study-study-study!"

"I love Principal Peaks," Ari said excitedly. "She's so cool!"

"Cool?" Cairo yelled. "I don't know about cool. She's really nice though, and she for sure has crazy energy all the time. And you can tell she loves us, kids!"

"I'd like to race," Ricardo said to his new best friends.

"You race?" Cairo asked, looking surprised.

"Are you fast?" Ari chimed in.

"I was pretty fast at my old school. I'm for sure an athlete," Ricardo answered.

"Well, we will see what you can do this Friday! Let's go get you signed up right now!" Ari said with enthusiasm.

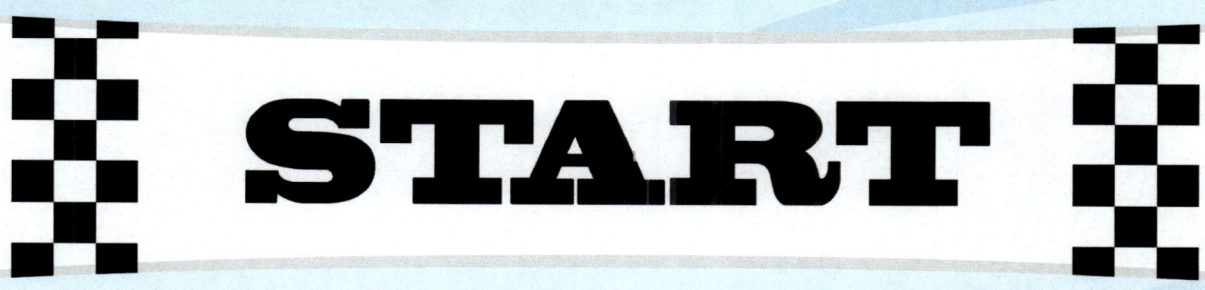

"On your mark," Principal Peaks said. "Get set... BANG!"

The races had been going on for what seemed like all day. But finally, all the top racers were preparing for their turn.

"You're going down!" Jace yelled at one kid who was stretching and getting ready for the race. "And you too, Billy!" Jace said as he shoved past him.

"Now remember your breathing, Cairo," Ari whispered. "Watch for Jace's accidental elbow as well."

As Cairo, Jace, and the other kids prepared for the race, Ari saw Ricardo eating a Twinkie and drinking some pop.

"Ari, did you see that?" Cairo said.

"Cairo, did you see that?" Ari replied. "This kid can't be eating all this bad food and call himself an athlete. There's no way he can be serious right now."

As the runners lined up for this huge battle of champions, Jace bumped into Cairo intentionally and said, "Oh, excuse me, Ro. If you were really fast, you could have moved out the way just now. But you're slow. Good thing I'll be way ahead of you during the race, so I will be safe from your clumsy feet."

"Man, you just stay over there. I'm coming for you today," Cairo snapped back to Jace.

Jace stepped on another racer's toes and pretended it was an accident. "Oops," he said, then made a mean face at other kids getting ready to start.

Ricardo also stepped up to the line. Other racers were looking at him, confused because he was the new kid.

Nobody had seen him run before or even knew why he was put in the race with the fastest kids.

Earlier that day, Principal Peaks had spoken to Ricardo. She told him that he would be placed in that race because she heard how fast he was from his old principal at his other school.

"Who's this kid?" Tano said to Jace, pointing at Ricardo. Tano was one of Jace's best friends. She was also very quick, but she ended up in third behind Cairo in most races.

"He's that new kid," Jace said. "Well, today he's gonna also be the last kid." He and Tano slapped high fives and started laughing.

As the kids all lined up, ready to go, they heard the command.

"On your mark... BANG!"

All the kids began running their hardest immediately. Cairo got his normal great start; he was pushing up towards the front of the group, and he could see Tano slightly to the left of him. She was running hard, but she was falling slowly behind. On his other side, Cairo could see Jace ahead of everyone. Jace was running with such ease. He looked like he would easily win another race.

Suddenly, something was coming up on Cairo's right side. Who could that be? He thought. Before he could look over to see who it was, he could already see the back of Ricardo's head.

"WHAT!" Cairo said out loud. Man, Ricardo is moving, he thought. Not only had Ricardo passed him, but Cairo saw that Ricardo was gaining quickly on Jace.

How fast the students raced. Oh, how fast.

"In front is Jace, as usual, in fourth place is Tano, and in third is Cairo," Principal Peaks announced. "But who is that in second and quickly gaining on first place? It is Ricardo!"

Shocked and amazed, Jace looked back to see someone coming closer, and closer, and closer! Jace pushed with everything he had in him. Then Ricardo pushed with everything he had in him. Ricardo caught all the way up to Jace. He was now running almost right next to Jace.

The two were so close to tying, but when the ribbon tore, everyone could see that Jace was still the fastest in the land.

"Better luck next time slugsters," Jace said to the other racers. Then he danced around the field, holding his medal and rapping:

> "I'm the best in the land;
> you can see it on my face.
> I'm faster than all of you clowns,
> and you will never beat Jace"

"I had no idea you had that in you!" Ari yelled while running up to Ricardo.

"Thanks, but I have not lost a race in a long, long time. I have never run that hard before. I don't think I can beat Jace," Ricardo said sadly.

"Don't you dare say that, Ricardo!" Ari screamed back. "You actually can beat him! I remember my brother Kaleb used to say, "The win will go to the most prepared person.' He used to work out, and I would watch him train so I'd know how to help other guys."

Ricardo looked up, excited to hear about the magic potion that she would give him.

"I know three things that could help you beat him, Ricardo!" Ari shared. She was so excited about seeing how fast Ricardo was. "First of all, watch what you eat. You eat junk, and you expect to be an athlete? That crap doesn't do anything positive for your body." Now she was in her coach stance. She had her hand on her hip and was waving her finger at Ricardo.

"So, you have to eat better. Secondly, you have to train and work hard. I can help you start the race strong." Ari was so energetic in her explanation that others besides Ricardo began to listen. "If you didn't have to catch up with everyone, you would have already been in the front during the race.

Your start was slow, so you lost a lot of time there. And third" now she was on a roll "you have to be able to fight. Dig deep and know that you can beat Jace."

'Don't focus on him," Ari continued. "Focus on the best version of Ricardo. We want to see that superior version of you racing in the next race. Trust me, make these changes and we will see your Superior Self win this race!"

Over the next few weeks, Ricardo took Ari's advice. He changed the way he ate. He would bring apples to school for his lunch. He would pack carrots and some celery along with ranch dressing to dip them in. On some occasions, he would also pack a small salad with some pepperoni slices mixed in. That was his pizza substitute.

After school, Ricardo would meet up with Cairo and Ari, and they would practice and practice. They worked so hard and not only did Ricardo's race time improve, but so did Cairo's. Cairo began to take his efforts to a higher level. He started taking the training more seriously since Ricardo did.

Ricardo was a new kid! He was eating better, he was getting faster starts, and so his confidence grew. He wasn't able to celebrate yet, because he knew that Jace had been the fastest for so long.

Finally, it was the day of the next race! Everyone had been talking about it. People were cheering for Jace, and others were cheering for Ricardo.

Even Kaleb came out to the race. Ricardo's big brother Ron and their mom came out to the race to watch and cheer. Ricardo's mom was so proud of how Ricardo had faced his fears he had, because of the move, and confronted dealing with his emotions in a positive, productive way.

She was proud that he worked so hard training to fight for his new goal.

As the runners lined up for the race, the crowd grew louder and louder.

"You ready to lose again, loser?" Jace yelled over at Cairo. "And your best friend Ricardo is going to get smoked just like you!"

Cheers rang throughout the stadium. "Let's go, Jace!" and "Let's go, Ricardo!" cheers could be heard streets away.

"Runners, take your mark," Principal Peaks said over the PA system. "BANG!"

The runners took off. This race was different than the race the previous month. This time there were three people who shot out to the front of the group of runners. In the lead was Jace, but Cairo was on his left side. Although Cairo was very close to him, Jace laughed at him and ran faster. Cairo started to get left behind.

What Jace didn't count on was the great start that Ricardo had. While focusing on Cairo, Jace didn't see Ricardo right next to him, on his right side. The two of them battled it out. Their arms pumped so fast that it was almost as if they both began to fly off the track. Neither one of them had ever run this fast before. The crowd was impressed at what they were watching.

Soon they both would be running through the ribbon. Jace pumped his arms a little harder, then Ricardo pumped his even harder.

Ricardo took the lead! He was in front of Jace finally. These two were so far ahead of everyone and were only a few steps from finishing.

Just a few yards before the finish line, Jace tripped and slowly fell to the ground.

This is it, Ricardo said to himself. I'm about to beat this bully! I am going to run through the ribbon, and I will be the fastest kid in the school. I'm going to rub it in Jace's face.

As soon as he had that thought, he remembered his brother Ron telling him to be a good sport.

Just because I'm the fastest in the school, doesn't mean I should be mean to other people. Treat others how you want to be treated, he thought to himself. Being fast makes me special, but everyone is special in some way, even Jace.

Just before crossing the finish line, Ricardo stopped and ran back to get Jace off the ground. Jace was extremely sore and could barely run. His muscles were so tired. Ricardo told Jace to lean on him so they could both take the last few strides and finish the race together.

The crowd was confused when they first saw Ricardo stop. Some were yelling, "Go, finish him." Then it got really quiet. Everyone watched Ricardo do something they had never seen before. Ricardo showed compassion for Jace. The crowd saw a student stop running, sacrificing the victory to go back to help another racer.

So there they were, hobbling those last few steps, getting to the ribbon. Both Jace and Ricardo crossed the finish line together.

"Thank you," Jace said to Ricardo.

"Of course. You would have done it for me, right?" replied Ricardo.

"Well, no. I wouldn't have, in the past. But now, I will help others in the future," answered Jace.

They slapped fives, and the two of them each got first-place medals. Everyone said that they were both the fastest kids in the school.

~The End~

I AM IMPORTANT
I AM VALUABLE

I THINK BEFORE I SPEAK
I THINK BEFORE I ACT

I DESIRE TO BE MY BEST
I DESIRE TO HELP THOSE AROUND ME

BECAUSE OF THIS:
I IMPROVE MY SURROUNDINGS!
THEREFORE I AM SUCCESSFUL

THEREFORE WE WIN!

We encourage you to say this pledge as often as you can, weekly, or even daily!

For more information about the "We Win Pledge" and how youth's lives across the country are being changed, you can reach us online at www.SeanGary.com.

Made in the USA
Middletown, DE
24 November 2025